Quotes
and
Poems
by a
Nobody

SUNNY REY

GARDEN OAK PRESS

GARDEN OAK PRESS
1953 Huffstatler St., Suite A
Rainbow, CA 92028
gardenoakpress.com
gardenoakpress@gmail.com

© Sunny Rey   All rights reserved

No part of this book may be reproduced, stored in a retrieval system or transmitted by any means without the express written consent of the author.

First published by GARDEN OAK PRESS   10/01/2013

ISBN-13: 978-1492747390
ISBN-10: 1492747394

Printed in the United States of America

The views expressed in this collection of poems are solely those of the author and do not necessarily reflect the views of the Publisher and the Publisher hereby disclaims any responsibility for them.

```
                    Date Due
            ─────────────────────
              
            OCT MAR      1983
            2|06  Trinity 9/13 Strummer
            3/12  Garrett/Mom & Dad
            sibs / Jenni/Bill Harding
            Jean E. & Marie C. Whit
            Facebook.com/Sunny-
            rey.t
            Sunnyrey.tumblr
```

          COUNTY PUBLIC LIBRARY

✳ A Very Special Thank you to 'Friends of the Poor'
✳ for all the wonderful work you have done in
   Nigeria, Africa www.FriendsofthePoorAfrica.org ✳

iii

Dear Reader,
This is a very lucky copy of a copy, that was written just for you. After all, the story can't write itself.
I love you already,
Sunny

Quotes and Poems by a Nobody

Sunny Rey

Garden Oak Press
Rainbow, California
gardenoakpress.com

Table of Contents

POEMS

Get Gone	3
Exit	4
To Transform	5
I Will Take This Back in Two Minutes, Read Now	6
How I Prefer Them	6
Compliments	7
Physiology	8
The day has come	9
If	9
My Older Sister	10
I Have Fallen in Love Again	11
Dressing Up	12
I	13
The Night Got Quiet	14
Legacy	15
Small Spaces	16
Spring	17
The Road Taking Form into Everything	18
Recap	19
The Day I Killed a Mediocre Metaphor	20
Memorial Day	22
Side Note	23
Little One	24
How Are You?	25
The Time for Writing Has Come	26
Peace, Old Man	27
Not Interested	28
There Never Existed a Hello	29
I Wonder About You	30
Thank You Baby	31
Bathing	32

Do You Still Buy Books?	32
Meow	33
The Nothingness	34
The Miles Between	35
Hum	36
The Wait	36
Seconds Please	37
And Here It Comes	37
In This Place	38
Menu	39
It Bothers Me	40
And There You Are and There You Go	41
For Moon's Sake	42
Today	43
To Kris	44
Tell Me About Her	45
Calendars	46
B	48
Echoed Knock	50
The Other Memories	50
And So I Am Told	51
Matchstick	52
How it is	54
It's Been a Long Long Time Since	55
I Just Wanted Someone to Grow Old With	56
Delete Debt	57
Shithead	58
The Way He Liked It	59
I Am Afraid	60
Why Didn't You Let Me Know?	61
I'm Over and Done	62
I Never Felt So Bad	63
Nothing in Common	63
The Haunting	64
Monsters	66
Consequence	66

I'm Gonna Be Fine	67
Seatbelt On	68
I Used to Give All My Love Away	68
It's All There	69
He Is the Best Thing	70
Unstartled	71
Risky Business	72
New Year's	73
I Can't Enjoy This	74
Adieu	75
The Raw Honesty of Ugly	76
Ending Hymn	76
Type X	77
I Haven't	78
Dodge	79
Hinge	80
Bridge Over Moat	81
Applause	82
Rotation	82
In the Distance	83
Forget Me Not	84
I Remember	85
Don't Prostitute Your God to Me	86
What It Will Do	86
Dilemma	87
I Miss My Sister	88
All the Futures I Made	88
Break	88
November 25	89
Wee	90
We Are	90
Shelter Me, Lover	91
It's Expired	92
Over the Mountain and Through the Dawn	93
The Viewing	94
< You	95

Chalkboard	96
Arm's Length	96
Dammit	97
Think About It	98
Sunday Night	99
October 1st	100
Discard	100
I'm Not Interested in the Person You Are Aiming to Become	101
Damn Me	102
Sometimes You See It	104
48 Hours	104
In the South	105
To a Chair in Hawaii	106
"Here lies another case of broken heart"	107
People Are So Painful	108
Fishing	108
To Nobody (all million of you)	109
Ring Toss	110
Growing up	110
The Drugs You Take	111
Themes	111
Life in the Current	112
Straddling the Noose	113
I Am Not Easy to Surprise	114
Same War	115
Bull Fighting	116
As For Me	116
The Recall	117
Grade C	117
And They Judge Us	118
Transgender	120
Second Thoughts	121
The Dentist	121
Found Out	122

Motherhood	123
Blues	124
These Gods Are Relentless	125
My Misfortune Pays Your Salary	126
I Struggled with Writer's Block Once	128
My Parent's Dog Is Moaning	129
Your Socks Filled with Criticism	130
I Broke You, Huh?	131
Shoreline	132
Night One	133
Empty Arena	134
Warning	135
I Am Poet	136
Dear Denny	137
I Cannot Convince Another	138
Time Flies When You're Swatting	139
Some Are Born Mid-Soar	140
It Happens That Way	142
I Am Still Afraid	143

QUOTES   145

POEMS

Everlasting Psychobabble

Get Gone

Needed to get gone from the traffic conversation
release faces, paging faces
notifications
judgments
eager eyes to meet my eager lips of ideas
just clear
singular oneness
I drew the lines that separates
divides

They can stay in the stands, the bleachers, the aisles
I will dig my stubborn head in the sand
and replace eyes with marbles
I will offer no more of my words
my writings
thoughts
pen imprint on paper

except after this one
And possibly the one after that

Exit

I drove thru Jack in the Box
for a fill up on lemonade (skip on the meal side)
and pulled out and collected my stray trash

I looked up and caught the gaze
of an old man in the middle of the restless street

He was stumbling
and puzzled over
his next move

But it looked like so much more than that
as if it wasn't the road
the passing hell-bound cars
the honks, stares
or flying single fingers in the air
It wasn't the *how*
It was the *where*

Holding his pants up by the crotch
grasping desperately to his 24-pack of Bud
as though he held tightly the secrets of the universe
under his brown-spotted arm

I drove away before he crossed
It pained me to see him
his blue cloudy cataract eyes desperate like that

I wonder if he ever did cross
ever figured out where he was going with those secrets
ever made it out alive

Do any of us make it out alive?
And when we do, are we old enough
to have secrets escorting us to our Exit signs?

To Transform

The trick is to not stay still
or to strike off full speed ahead
but rather turn   sideways
dart
glide
hurry
remove and step
sideways
a little distance
and make room for forgiveness
a little space
to stare over at yourself
and take inventory from this vantage point
turn sideways
not through to get through
sideways
to trick yourself out of denial
stare your old selves down
until they're the ones running out of
town
Turn sideways
Stay available
Change is never too far

I Will Take This Back
in Two Minutes, Read Now

I don't want to be this storm
this cancer strutting up inside you
I'm sorry I truly am
I hope she makes sweet love to you, I really do, I really do
You're the star hovering over someone else's twelve moons
High time I stop wishing on you
Love you enough to set you free
Quickly go
sustain life
far from where I can get to you
Can't trust my yearning selfish need

How I Prefer Them

I like them intense
limited on substance
The types who aren't heard
but rather felt
from the heat fanning off the fire in their gut

Lit up like an infirmary of madmen
burning pages of nothing into dust
words exhaust too quickly
Fire walks all over what words stumble on talk

Compliments

Dammit he isn't calling
and I know why
No
not because I fucked him on the first go
not because I paid for the last two drinks
and danced on barstools
and signed my autograph on my bra for his roommate
or because of the blood spot on his whites
not because he wanked it to finish
or because I stunk in the morning of wine
not the zombie walk-of-shame
with the skirt pulled up
and the lipstick-smeared smile to his Ma on my way out

It is because I told that son-of-a-bitch in between shots
that I thought he was really something

Now that hot shot inflated balloon-head is off
being something
to a new someone

while this somebody is banging her head
remembering never to sleep with compliments
on the first date

It takes time for them
to un-deserve all those mistaken phrases
you almost said

Physiology

Heart jumps to chest
chest rises
sinks deep, deep down
turning in
away from pain
when last night, outward similar motion
chest rises
rests in
anticipates the rise again
as I climax on you
Love making
Satisfaction
Tonight left with the aftermath reaction
Rejection
Disappointment
Self-doubt
Chest sinks in
caves in
collapses to memories of you

The Day Has Come

The day has come when the burning sun
heated the tranquil amnesia
and shot it off like a gun
into the center where once so much startled pain had begun
Oh, the day
the sweet compassionate day
Rest arrived as promised
and I am no longer tired
energized with please
easing into the day
Oh, the day has come
arriving to replace all others
the bullets being cocked into tomorrow
swinging over the horizon
of a future the past cannot crash into (in two)

If

If you hadn't lied
If I hadn't lied
If you had waited
and I had not insisted
If never the twins
court
money stress
holiday stress
ex-lovers that really weren't technically ex
If   If   If
If it wasn't that
it would have been some other listed *if*
Unless, if . . .

To My Older Sister

Where did you go?
Here you stand with holes poking through your veins
Finally able to see you
you finally stand translucent
I am able to see tiny dots of blue and green
marking one scar for each past childhood haunting
Where are you tonight?
Are you under me in the ground I stand above?
Are you above me flying off to the clouds, the stars
to the god we lost?
Where are you?
Who are you?
Why?
Why must some be doomed
created in
and continue to create so much
intense
 powerful
frightening
and paralyzing
pain?

I Have Fallen in Love Again

I have fallen
again   again and again
in love
with this man
this man who I have met and re-met
in all lightings of the fluorescent-structured street sun
I have seen him glow under and outshine
only to quiet down in the evening
turning half his face away into a shadow
Under the breeze of an after-dusk book
I have heard him
for the first time   many times
and taken many notes on the depths of decimals in his breaths
I have fallen
hard   so hard
I hit our love
and I have fallen softly   so softly
I wondered if he knew I had approached at all
And now
I have fallen
in what I already accept to be
a state rather than a phase
and I see myself
twirling through the top of a sky
that has bottomed out
with the most glorious smile
I have ever felt my face stretch into

Dressing Up

In the life of a poet you can find me hanging from a tree
examining its branches as I participate in the breaking
Every time you see me I wear a different coat
It is as if I am walking among you, eerie as a ghost
I paint pictures of characteristics you fancy in yourself
just to walk by you
to be near you
to watch your world
Then I leave
retire to a typewriter
and sing about you
take bits and pieces of you
I am seen as so sociable
but it takes weeks, not hours to leave my house
I am so tempted by the allure of my own company
it is hard to stay with the living
or to motivate the changing
of yet another coat

I

I saw a 32-year-old man call himself old
and mean it
I saw a man forget the lyrics to his own songs
apologize to strangers for fucking up
interrupting their awe with apologies felt
as painful as watching that teacher
I had as a high school sophomore
make two to three daily remarks
about how his wife recently left
how his son was on meth
and his mother in hospice
It's just sobering and uncomfortable
to have your happy view of someone's life
intruded on by their reality
The way student voices soften
their hearts soften
in a desk
or smoking pot at a show
when these annoyances of familiar
relatable feelings by gods are expressed
If we are quiet enough
we can hear the hymn
of our own internal dialogue
apologizing for becoming what we all
promised never to grow up into
I'm 29
I'm fucking old
And I'm sorry

The Night Got Quiet

My mind was on timeout
It was raining relentless showers
with intervals of teasing whistles of wind
My Internet failed
and I sat uneasily on my couch
sunken like a seatbelt at the moment of impact
Uncomfortably snug
I had nothing to distract my head
too lazy from this paralyzing depression
to search out a book to read
to get lost in
And that's when I thought of you
and a collection of recent to lifetime ago lovers
and how you all have found your glove of a love
while I sit and write about my loneliness
Will there ever be that comfortable one for me?
Why does it seem
after me
you all move on to *the one?*
And I watch it all
I watch it all
One after another
the *one*   the *one*   the *one*
while I am so obviously set aside
and remembered as the one you tried on
before you found
your one

Legacy

120 pages
That sounds like a good book
Right now I'm looking at half that
(when doing the math in my favor)

It's not that I am necessarily eager
to parade for the stick figures
to receive bullshit remarks on my "work"

Today is just one of those times
I wished for a veil to hide behind
Most complain of labels
though "published poet" on a jar of me sounds pretty delicious

I need to be someone
a Miss So-and-So today

Like a goofed up hat worn on holiday
I will wear it once
be photographed in it just once
Then when I am old
I will pull out the crusty album
and show it off to my grandkids and say
"See, look at that goofy hat I wore
I sure was somethin' wasn't I"

Small Spaces

Verdict in
papers finalized
We have failed each other
our vows
Face forward, staring at a forecast of pain
this new forced-formed reality
living without you center-folding my life

So haunted by worry for you
I was left unattended
The hurt from you
filled up the space left
for the definition of me

What happened to the marriage of the in-between

Dinner party for one
food for thought
with a dine-and-ditch discount on my watch

Spring

It takes
It takes so little
It takes everything
while it takes so little

He can get away
and he does
get away
on, oh so little
while taking it all

He says three words
three small words
and there it goes
out the door
along with those words
my heart

It takes
It takes so little
It takes everything
while it takes so little to take it

The Road Taking Form into Everything

Before him
dim lighting
tripping on my own feet
distracted by flies
and spooked by my shadow underneath

Then sunshine

You filled the forest
The roots of ancient trees began to glow
You perked up the leaves
and cast their slumbering arms in glory

You found me
just as I was saying out loud
"I'm lost"

You were the thing I held on to
when I was alone
Your road crossed mine
We became an eight
circling
and flirting at small distances
just to circle around
and meet in the center to resume again

And this eight moved us through the forest like a wheel
And with you
and this movement
the light of the future
rising out of the forest cave
bloomed again

I owe you everything   everything

If you had not come
I would have just stayed there
and rooted myself to a road that ended at the tip of my toe

I owe you everything for not leaving me in there alone
I owe you everything

Recap

What am I doing with my life?
I'm waiting to fuck
I'm waiting to shit
to drop pounds
to become a reflection
of unreal human beings on the covers of
magazines
I'm smoking in a tracksuit
American hypocrite

The Day I Killed a Mediocre Metaphor

Relationships work like zippers
You meet
notice you are both hanging free
available
You come together
and it fits
It's smooth and easy to retrace and cover and tour each other
through this gliding elevation of excitement
The experience goes up and down
dresses and undresses
over and over
sometimes done mindlessly in haste
other times bubbly and showing off
you move along its harsh ridges
and seek comfort when those ridges are covered again
until one day it doesn't zip
You are hopeful that it is just stuck again
(because recently it's been getting stuck more and more)
There are parts that come together
and yet there is this bigger part that does not
now causing a draft right through the center
You are stumped
This is what you have always done
Up   down   down   up
and now
a hole

So you tug on the hole
(knowing damn well that tugging only adds to the size)
tug until   *split*
ending up all the way down to where you started
You attempt to reconnect
(but your heart's not in it)
You take it off and hang it back up
thinking this will fix itself
but return to it a few more times
for the viewing
Same big
        split
And while observing the split
you note that the colors are faded
It really is looking rather drab
and after all, your friends have already seen you in it
you have been photographed wearing it over and over
It now, with time
seems less and less needed
You ditch the hanger and shove it far inside a junk drawer
until that drawer collects more broken zippers
Months later
inventory time
starting like the relationship started
empting the drawer out
bottom to top

Memorial Day

I thought going to the bookstore
on a crowded Saturday night Memorial Day weekend
would make me feel
a silent camaraderie

Instead I glance up from my book of Bukowski poems
 at the gaunt faces of the other losers

I am not comforted
I am embarrassed to be one of them

When the hell did this happen?
I was a looker
a conversationalist
had wads of cash in my wallet
and a personality worth gravitating to
a job to talk about
friends to introduce
goals   accomplishments   truths
an imagination wild enough to lie

Not now
No longer

I roll with:
Mr. and Miss Gut-Belly
Mr. Cargo Pants
Mrs. Standard Stock Cell Phone Ring
Mr. Socks With Sandals
Mr. Car Keys Jingling
Mrs. Books Listed On Oprah's Book Club Two Years Ago

I am somehow one of them

Fuck

At least I'm reading a book by a drunk

Better than Frost
Better than Sandberg
Better than Nin

At least my writer
the echo in my head
reading back at me these words I pick up by eye
at least he's angry

At least he's alive enough to be socially dead

Side Note

Do I look like I am waiting or avoiding?
For some reason this seems crucial

Sometimes it all hurts
must hurt
So you remember
enough to repeat
never again
not again

Little One

Every look
you have ever created
awes me
takes me back
Your brilliance
light
journey singular
yet my beaten path
somehow worthy of you
Whatever I ever did to deserve you
I wish I could pinpoint
and relive in Thank You's
Whatever I did to create space between
I repent and will undone
I will be
strive to
won't settle
better for you alone
I want to change the masses
for you alone
I wake, eat, rest and hit repeat
You have changed me
A stranger named me
raised me
but you alone claimed me
I was lost without you, dear angel
in search of completion
and there you manifested inside of me
symbolically becoming
my own answered prayer
And now to watch you
is to watch myself without a dirty face

And to raise you
ups all the stakes
I will make an example of what I hope for you
Give, give, give, little one

How Are You?

"How are you?"
he asked
"Great!"
I responded
not because I was great
but because I wanted him to think I was
great
and nothing short of that
but I forgot to mention the nothing-short-of part
(hopefully he won't catch on)
Truly great people, I bet, would never leave that out

The Time for Writing Has Come

Oh, it is indeed the time to write again
to let go of thoughts
We are far apart now
We indeed were once one skin
one beat of one thump
now different orchestras color our lives
never on the same note
never slowing to keep in sync
or even stopping our band for one moment
to see what tune the other is playing
You're playing in G while I'm impressed with C
What happened to *us*?
We are so normal now
We live leashed up in thoughts never shared
It is as though we are neighbors to our cells
We are sad to watch
running out of youth and days
oh, so common now
less than little to say
I wish to hug you in my words
to impress you
turn you on
but I have learned now
to retire instead here
to my paper, my computer, my diary
and toss out love into thin unreceptive air

Peace, Old Man Bukowski

It's another night that I'm digging Bukowski
Cursing lovers
and being horny just takes the shape of revenge
My gut is uneasy
unsteady in its usual state of aloneness
Tonight is its sadness's bi-annual greeting
where I tally up my pathetic grail
and play the baby violin for one
I need to refrain from hysterically laughing
or letting myself run rampant and mad
I adjust to the sensation of my shadow on the wall
and look at it nodding and taunting
Tonight we gather together to fall
Peace be to the bitter who can't stop cramping their fingers
to continually objectify
Peace be to the angered who could be victims no longer
and sit silently as their lovers love others and lie
And peace be to me and the beast that dwells within me
feeding off memories that were never mine really
Peace be to this night and that old man Bukowski
who, I hope, I hope, after all that tragedy in his poetry
crept quietly, sagged happily to his whorehouse in the sky

Not Interested

I'm not interested in meeting someone new
I protested
It is you!
It is YOU I have been waiting for
calculating for
debating, celebrating, dieting, coloring my hair, my skin
into tan
all in anticipation for this
this coming
not this going
Please don't come to pass
Last
Last!
Be the last
Be the last I dream up
the dream that takes flight
Fly
Unhook your anchored wings
I promise not to hurt you
What I request in this participation of waiting in between
is that all cargo of doubt be tossed overboard
It will sink us
We will drown
Believe me
I am not interested
in anymore of the musing around
I am not interested in much at all
if you are not a part of it
In you all possibilities birth
Let's make thousands of memories
and raise them like children
Be my new family

I am not interested in less
unless
you are not interested at all

There Never Existed a Hello

I no longer blister and bleed nails into
all that vanished long ago
I refuse to hold down what's been let up
I will not chase the vanishing trail I mistook for a road
I won't mourn the death of the fantasies wept
when a priest can't be convinced to show
I cannot twist my guts into enough knots
to validate the pain of loss that was not
and when I say goodbye I must admit
there never existed a hello
Nothing will ever be this real again
because all the knowing is left
for the dead

I Wonder About You

Still
I wonder
if you will write, text, call
change your relationship status
think of me
dream of me
crave   yearn   need   me

think of my daughter
miss us
want us
more than her

What was so wrong
so unbearable
so unworkable
so horrible

about your life with me
about me
about you being here

today   tomorrow
just
couldn't stomach it?

God, how could I have been so wrong
so self absorbed?

I was happy with you
You are happy with her

Thank You, Baby

Steadiness
stillness
is conceived in the corners of her lips tilted up to the heavens
Her smile
breaks the mold of my frown
With her I am genuine
With her I am impressed
What honest arms
the only one I have ever known
to cause no pain
Because she needs me
I need me
What otherwise may be a life without will
I will it every day
Her tiny life makes my life
My daughter
dear comfort
dearest trueness
the value of my gratitude is priceless
Thank you
Thank you
Thank you

Bathing

I took a bath
My skin is still overheating
The hot water steamed my pores
I feel at one, surrounded by water
In this tub I am home
disappointed again by the recall
that once my fingers wrinkle
and my soft skin turns dehydrated
it is the last grain in the hourglass
and up and out I go
stepping out slowly from my Caribbean waterbed
and on to the dingy floor grassed with gunk
yet again reminded of my reality
No purity or baptism is left

Do You Still Buy Books?

"Do you still buy books?"
I asked him last night after round two
"Yes," he said
"but I read these days mostly from my iPad"
"Oh"
"Why?" he responded
"No reason"
I lied

(I asked because I needed to know
where to sell my book where he could find it)

I hope he gets it

and gets the book after that

Meow

Sly kitty cat
you twist your curls
stranded on your face
You know me well, silent friend
You creep
crawl
in my uneasy direction
walk with me
distracting my crooked road
purr when I find righteousness
and distance yourself as I damage my youth
find yourself a distracted string to play with
as I cry
myself
to sleep
in a ball hugged tighter
and smaller
than your silhouette

The Nothingness

I try so hard to sit still
close my eyes and empty
let go
drain the drought of tears built back
all in attempt
to release
detox
guilt   sin   shame
But just when I reach out to it
the nothingness
the lack of gravity under my longing
unsteadies these emotions
I cry
I cry so hard   Sob
I inhale
and see your face
I exhale in this safe place
You stand there
threatening my peace   this closure
All attempts to move forward are impeded
they are rain-stormed with memories
of you under a steamed window
huddled in the heat of the bath
you hold me backwards in to you
into all of your viewed perfection
The bar of passion is set so high
I blink
you're gone
the past fast-forwards into the present

and I am still reaching out in to the nothingness

The Miles Between

Because your face was like home
and I'm stuck drowning under layers of suffocating blue
watching you in shimmery spurts
moments briefing
as though you're the sun taunting over me
leaving me foolishly with your room to hope
that this is not damning
but rather a choice
as though I could swim up to you
and embrace your warmth and end this painful longing
this nauseous homesick feeling
like being sea sick
it comes in relentless waves
with every picture
every memory
every word of your whereabouts
mention of your name
pain pulls my heart
a want pierces through me
guts anchor to the floor
left so embarrassing translucent
a stranger could swim straight through me
and yes I stay here
below
dark in the satin layers of navy
and bubbly clear frozen ocean
so isolated in the absence of your vessel
watching you like yellow diamonds above me
you come and you go
I cowardly drift by and by

Hum

When we first met
that song played, turned it up to ten
I think of you on hot days

Not asking much
just for you to be the songbird to my melodies

Here in the passengerless car I hum and I whistle
but it doesn't come in full bloom
I can't remember the words
without your lips leading me into submission
guiding me to the catchy chorus everyone should know

At least once in their lives, they deserve to feel such a tune

The Wait

Love find me here
I will freeze myself to make easy your search
I won't burden you with stairs
I am humbled on begging knees
You have a free pass to enter into my sleep
shoot across my thoughts
see my desires and dreams of you
trapped in timeless butterflies
meet just my glance
brush against my shoulder
cross the bridge at noon
I will meet you
need you
want you
choose you
Choose me

Seconds Please

Can't recite it quite as well as you said it
but unbearably positive you placed hidden daggers there
in those words you spoon-fed to me
telling me everything I was hungry to receive

Starving again until I finish my time machine back to that day
where you echoed into my quietest corners

Until I get back to you
I will be picking at crow's feet
eating up every lie the world offers me
remembering what you gave me

Something more

I need more of that

And Here It Comes

Brad Renfro died last year, two days before my birthday
My sister's down to her last hit
She's next any day now
The world is spinning out of control
while some walk around smiley
and content with contemplating
their next show on TV
their next microwaved meal
followed by a McDonald's drive-thru cone
I lie awake at night and think of how the hell I'm gonna afford
the expense of her funeral
as the movie, *The Cure*, sings me to sleep

In This Place

People have halos 'round their heads
confusing the shadows under wings
Might it be mirrored reflections
of all the aftermath consequences
or an understatement for the impending doom
which looms from your greedy heart stringing me along?
The time passes slowly when you're using
what is left for the taking

Locked in rooms of lavender and bones
scattered over withered idols and religious statues

You love me hard then leave me tingled, frayed and alone
Do they ever stay?
Better catch left for another day
When skipping rocks over shallow waters
you sink fast and slow
Find me a way to the ocean deep
with room enough to submerge and get lost into myself
where I host rooms in me that protect you

Find me the one that sleeps under the skies that bleed
We can soak our skin clean there
from the filth of the world aglow

The shadows of wings can soar above us
as we repeat the vow to love each other more

Menu

There are more drugs in the meat at the market
than in the pills I take
I am at a place of self-hatred
denial
pause
I feel isolated
saddened
stuck
Drugged by the supermarket
the people
the prices
the stress of it all
Just roll them up and put them in the revolver
one by one
Russian roulette
they come   keep coming
I anticipate the hit to end it
one less disease-infested flesh
filling up the aisles of the store with miles of regret

It Bothers Me

It bothers me when people say we entered this world
alone
as though that is reasonable justification for my loneliness
my tallied-up holidays spent singular
My tears
they are understated
they are
unwarranted
I should hush it
and accept it
that we entered alone
quiet
stay put
be ok with
swallow it
that I very may well die alone
the way I entered

When in truth that is not how it happened at all
I entered at one with my mother
I was *inside* someone
depending on her for all nourishment
for sustainability
If she did not eat
I did not
If she chose to take her own life
and die
I too would fade
Every song she sang
I heard
and felt her vibrations beat all around me
I was nestled safe within her vessel
a consistent drum playing becoming my lullaby to sleep

And then the day came when we were to detach
and not for one second did I go unwatched or unheld
or unlooked at   or unloved   or unfed

Until adulthood
until divorce
until he stopped loving me
and until I stopped believing in people

And it is very unnatural
very uncomfortable
being alone
and being told it should not bother me
It does

And There You Are
and There You Go

I wanted so sincerely for our lives
to intertwine
harmoniously in sync and rhyme
but the colors of your intense blue
and my passive yellow
won't blend
Feels more like a bleeding
a knife
separating
always on the outside of your life

And there you are and there you go

For Moon's Sake

Close them tight
Right there with you
wrapped and loved and embraced by you
Effortlessly we coast right through
the illusion that held us back at daybreak
For my lover's sake
the visit spent in silence
for we have overstepped word limits
in the past visits allotted
I transcend your gaze
multiply my natural state
by the comfort of this vessel
I dwell safe inside
I cling to the moment
as we approach the tickings
and beatings
and shoutings of the clock
A single tear streams down my face
It collects with the puddle I've collected in this state
It's coming now
I wrestle to control it
No brakes are released
so I realize
I abide   I obey
I take a small step away from you
and your head tilts up
so that my desperate eye will align
with your blues and greens
I blink
I awake from safety to sleep
I settle into my space
and I realize in this place I was replaced

You are off loving new lovers
I am here torturing my sunshine
and yearning for starlight

When will you come again, dear illusion
dear intangible thing?
The healing to hurt
the subsiding of frustrations
in all deceptions will ease
if you could just meet me
Please meet me in sleep

Today

Today I promise to hit the damn print button
to slouch
to drink
to down some pills
and drown my ears with music
as I never lift up to check my previous sentence
hit the keys with passion
and spell some shit wrong
(that's what smart computers are for)

Today I will just write and print
print and sort through
the thoughts I have neglected
the funerals I have yet attended
for the past writings never printed

To Kris

But then again
I'm on my period and shouldn't promise feelings I can't
or won't
allow myself to feel tomorrow
but I want you
I want even harder to tell you
to stay
that I love you
and I am so in need of the even exchange in that phrase
to be wrapped up in your soft-spoken blues
A whisper that hugs me   secures me
safely hushing a loneliness
I didn't know I was feeling
until I had your company
to hold up next to
the stark contrast
of life before
and life in this moment with you
I'm terrified and stumped by myself
What is it I educatedly
and articulately am asking for –
to take your freedom?
Family man you?
All for me
to feel free
What a selfish single mother
I must quiet this yearning
to trip you up
I must staple my lips
and cracks in my center
Go back
Just me   just me   just me

Tell Me About Her

I fucked up but I'm confessing it now
please forgive me
You must
forgive me
When life robs you from living
secret lives worn tight
judgments
misconceptions
our own projections
prejudices
bags over the faces
of people we will never allow ourselves to know
swayed like a tree
until you get that solid core rooted
to withstand the rough wind
I have been blind
living a lie
If I ever allowed myself to de-mask
I wouldn't recognize my own face

Did I ever?
Did you know her?
Me?
What was she like to you?
That me, that I will never know
Tell me about her

Did she sway from her branches to and fro?

Calendars

I can't do it
spend another year
setting out pumpkins
carving the tofurkey
setting out lights
baskets
candy grams
birthday balloons
alone
I need a partner
to walk through life with
to raise my daughter with
supply my oxygen
dance in to our 30s, our 50s
our silver, our gold anniversaries
graduations
deaths
witness more births
practice conception every night in the heat of sheets
My daughter deserves the best
which I fear I am not alone
Not another year
not one more frustration
of fighting tears
while sorting through bills
going cuffed into debt
making promises I kill myself to keep
I am not enough
for my perfect baby

I need a steady friend
turned lover
into stepfather
complete what has been broken
and never swept up
though trashed
The life I signed up for
made promises in
was ripped away from us
me and her
Help paint not just the fence
but the picture I have outlined
The colors inside this frame
are bleeding together
into brown   into black
as my heart yearns
 turns   tosses
loses sleep
over the waiting for you

B

What's happening to me?
You   you have taken over
you are nestled in every cell
every heartbeat
every breath inside of me
I have whispered the words
"I love you"
dozens of times today
after only one night
one one-on-one connection
I am so devoted to you
amazed by you
insanely, unjustifiably
head over toes mad for you
I close my eyes
to recreate
the moments
the breaths before
the longing sensations
of insisting lips
the fire of tongue
my body in melted form
you solid as a rock
I form to you
and you to me
and we unite
and I hold you there
in this place
past the hours of the night
into the night to come
and waves of thoughts
and the fantasies of next time
next   and after that

I long for the buildup of the moments before you enter
the moment before you love me back
the vows I replay
 I surrender
I have completely lost it
I am giving in to the imagination
I retreat to the dorms of my youth
in my mind
on holiday
painting lovely pictures
of the life I choose to live
the man I long to live with
I will cowardly turn my back on the reality
Here in this place I will stay
with you
your breath
your kisses
your tongue
youth
body
warmth
Stay
this way

Echoed Knock

I too still wonder
about the rooms of my soul
Where do the doors lead
and how about those deserted roads too?
What are my private intentions?
What is it that fills spaces between cells?
Fragments of generosity
stones made of viciousness?
Like the candles burning into the night
it is only a failed attempt at comfort
just as the false repetition of my heartbeat
has me defining that as the only proof I am
alive

The Other Memories

They attack like a draft
flowing by the right side of my mind's eye
and into the furnace
up through the belly of thick smoke
a fog of something darker than
blackness
turning into the shape of countless crows
gently releasing
from the gut
of this weight I carried
in the form of yesterday's shadowed ghost

And So I Am Told

that I am now ordinary
Such a word to choose for myself
when in a time not far from the present
I was viewed as your passionate freed spirit
You were jealous of me
When the night cloaked us
you gazed past shooting stars
to glimpse at me
I sang you a dream of the future of us
and you believed without question
but now
that cover
that awe
that mask
has cracked away
and over time
you see less
I dread the night
ashamed to fall asleep near you
afraid to witness you now
eyes pierced to the window of a hidden moon
you glance time to time mindlessly at me
searching
but find nothing deep

Matchstick

He can get matchsticks
to strike in wind
the same way he turns me on after the world switched me off
digging into blown-away pieces of myself
burnt-out ashes of my vessel flow fierce
burn bright back to life
on the very first try
created this moment to shine inside
what was years of a devastated pitch-black night
on the very first try
as though it was my first time

Now responsibility lies on my flimsy flame
to continue the fight
to keep believing that though I am light
I will not be burned to twigs
to nothing again

Don't burn away
or rush me out
Protect me
safe inside your warm sincere hands

Steady now
Stay

I flicker a little bigger
brighter
steady
against the winds blown from the shadows off
the passing people in the streets

They loom over us
attempt distraction
temptation
disconnection
false satisfaction

Stay with me

Choose this light
stay the keeper of our nights
Darling please
don't let me return to them
the shadows
the crowds
black and grey

Put me in color
Yellow
burning bright yellow

How It Is

The sun is too horny for my taste
hard up on heat intimidating me back to last night
lost romantic sights never to be seen again
I came out from hibernation
Was there for four draining years
afraid of the pain the day might hold for me
for in past days proven to be some sort of mind-fuck enemy
but then I saw his golden light
which increased my provocative curiosity when I heard
his crooked mouth speak
Like rays reaching out to me
I tiptoed away from hiding's safe space
and trusted   him
and this is what I get for that
Foolish girl like all the rest
come rushing full speed out of security
into the devious tempting arms of mystery
It's mysterious because it should be
I should have never made real a dream
because when you make real the sun
and get close enough to touch
and needy enough to attempt to obtain
you will reach out to it
and every time
every damn time
you will get burned

It's Been a Long Long Time Since

I've opened up and exposed and made room and let in someone
all for them to look at everything I have to offer
walk out of my heart and leave no sandbags
to cover the holes in the spaces they weighted down

How am I to trust myself again
how will I define the right time to show my insides
how will I label the same places in me
with the same self value as then
when
you are able to leave it
and me
with less than what I was
unable to stand up for myself or against the anchored wind?

You stole from me
the most precious locked up forgotten treasure
I had waited so long to offer

You took my faith
my core   my base

I am a hanging vacancy sign
hung over a parlor
where lovers use to live

I Just Wanted
Someone to Grow Old With

someone sweet
and comfortable
and still

I cared for you in the most honest way I knew how

I tried to leave no words unsaid
but never got to the "I love you's"
though I wrote them down
and spelled them out
and mouthed the words over your sleeping eyes

The time
wasn't yet right

And now
the time is up

It's so unfair
to outgrow this affair
before growing old
and dying alone here

Delete Debt

Everybody has a story and nobody owes you shit

Every girl has been hurt
every man stoned in upbringing

We will love
and we will betray one another
and it is no one's responsibility but ours alone
to mend together all the hurt
and frustrations
and illusions of being wronged

This whole place is a palace
a slate clean   ready to start fresh
no one but you as the creator
the destroyer
the chooser of your emotions
and reactive reactions to others illusions

This is your dream
This is your life

So love yourself right

Shithead

I bought a star for you

I bought it in memory of your deceased friend

I bought it to comfort you
to help you
to ease the knife of the night
and I tried guiding you upward
and pointing out a star
and imagined myself sliding
one of my hands
over one of your hands
and slowly pointing to the star

and I can almost feel
my heart smile

as I explained what I did just for you
"I bought you a star"
a moment in time
a piece of the universe
eternity

But you gave up on me
neglected me
forgot and moved away from me
before I got to give it to you

So at night
I cry
(only a little)

only when I look up
and see that damn star

an ornament of mockery
a silent statement of the state of my life

The Way He Liked It

He never wanted nothin' but to chase me

If I'd slow down and embrace the capture
he'd become scared and walk eerie backwards

He'd rather I be cleaning my bed sheets twice a week
than to be picking out curtains

He liked it that way
me that way
few steps in front of him
enough to where he could still see me
but my edges blurred out a little thin

I hurt less that way
(he hurts more then)

I Am Afraid

Not often do I admit it
and even more rare is it shared
for fear of spreading like cancer
for fear of becoming more aware

It is almost as though it's everything
BIG
and everything
small

I am afraid of it
afraid of it all

afraid of love
because it leaves with more than it gave

afraid of trust
because it twists your words

afraid of how these people lead to intimacy
these people lead to lust
then these emotions
that catalyze themselves back to love

Why Didn't You Let Me Know?

The language of your inner world
a place made up of watercolors
painted by a small child
you bleed from your page
all over my book

and it's getting weighted down now
and tough to carry

Because you came first
you are placed ahead of me
so all the trash you throw out your window
is then left for me

Even through nearly no contact
you dominate your demands

My dreams are then shelved
strapped inside bleacher stands
where I spend my life watching
your near-yawning script story
of a mother too involved with her boring pallet of colors
so she ran all over mine

And mine are left looking more like they're crying

Mother be kind to the bidding and buy

I'm Over and Done

Well that was fun
I'm done buying stars
and spending time in your bars
I know your house
I know your mouth
I know your kisses
your outer edges
what makes you tick
what makes you walk
(you've walked away before)
I know your limits
your lack of lust
this life with you with no warmth
no public touch
only behind doors
Do you score a charade of pretending to want more?
So judged around you
this never ending trial
I am prepared to plead guilty
just to get away from your strange city
where you refuse to hold my hand
give me more than simple conversation
a bit too much hesitation
I'm standing on the new ground of realization
what you got
I am not
and therefore do not want

I've Never Felt So Bad

in such a short amount of time
So lonely next to one man
who makes me feel translucent
short of worthy
of his attention and affection
likes to shake me up a bit
unstable and undefined
challenge me
and break and peck me apart
I will never return
to your abuse factory
where we quietly relive all the sweetness I give
that you return never
that I offered always
Never again

Nothing in Common

You left the door open
so I walked out

and when I did
I turned
and jerked around
for a final viewing of the paranoids
who dwelled behind windows
that were lined with iron

Bars on homes are for the paranoid

I prefer disco
I prefer clubs

The Haunting

I was reminded today that I am adopted

No other feeling quite as disturbing
and alarming
as the haunting
of the death and the longing
for a family of strange ghosts
who whisper for you
taunt away at you
show up
when you forget them

My guts anchor
cut like knives
and pain nestles inside vessels
where sweet nothings used to hide

It is like I'm trapped inside myself
searching and crawling
repeating, "Mother where are you?"

Down dark hallways in my mind
a quick shadow turns the corner
a demented low giggle right behind
"Mother is that you?"
Giggle, duck, dive around corners
she hides
and I curve and hug those corners
down labyrinths
She won't come out
She won't come out

And she doesn't always giggle
or reflect shadows
And those are the better days

Because I forget mid-search what I am in search of
like a dog forgets mid-chasing its tail
and I am able to stop the intense focused madness
and retreat to life's distractions
on daytime television

And there
between commercials
I hear it beating
My heart moans the dreaded meeting
of that giggle that has started again

Monsters

I have come across the most insensitive people
in the shortest amount of time
and the responsibility in knowing
I opened the door and invited the strangers in
and so they did
They walked in right through me
and took over the damn place
rumbled and shook storm damage
then fell fast into deep comfortable sleep
as I stay up cleaning up after the monsters
piece by piece
piece by piece

Consequence

I wrote him a poem
He sent it back
red-inked
corrected grammar

I wonder how he's doing
I haven't talked to him since

Maybe he found himself
a girl with a nice pink eraser
to piss away judgmental time with

I'm Gonna Be Fine

Nothing worse than a band-aid that won't peal
pulling while I still posses the strength
I go to count backwards from three
I grip and I tug
but buckle at the knees
What is it about you that's got me sewn shut?
You're not after all even open to my touch
and won't for the life of me let up
I fight but I'm weak
caused by your wreaked havoc beneath
You left me in ruin
forcing dreaded self-defeat
I cannot take it much longer
you're infecting too deep
I must detach now
before you take the core from me
I shut my eyes tight
knowing it hurts more to see you go
Two down to one, it's time now to go
I seek and I'm shocked when I look down in disbelief
that old painful wound
has now new skin underneath

Seatbelt On

Pedal slammed to the floor
punching out *accelerate*
searching for something more
My ego turned over
passed out in the back seat
next to numbness and grief
Things have taken a turn for us again
skid marks down skid row
in fury let you go
When you let me down I reach up to him
but in this equation
I start where I begin

I Used to Give All My Love Away

like an orphan left in a wicker basket
Come morning found myself in mercy's arms to a stranger
who found me deserted on a porch
I no longer seek out this set up
for imposing rejection
a reaction of attachment
brought on too fast and unwarranted
I now am patient and still
knowing there's nothing at all like the thrill
of being the one chased after
while you sit quiet and will everyday
to turn dreams
into confident manifestations
of home

It's All There

People are always mourning things they never had
relationships that never bore fruit
childhoods with absent parents present
the experience of success
in a dream they never put effort forth in

I don't think we as human survivors
are completely missing the mark
Perhaps there is therapeutic healing
in the reflection of what never was

If only we could harness those thoughts more directly
and set us up for something to feel gained

When daydreaming of the time we dodged homelessness
or bailed the relationship right before violence
for that time we never went hungry or without

It's all there
the wiring
We just need to bolt and fuse it
rearrange and adjust it
to become energized
as opposed to another drop in the bucket of nothing
or never was

Therefore: one never can be
when formed tirelessly the same way

He Is the Best Thing

What I have been asking for
Description fit the ad
He is darling with risky edges
   The best part of bad
And says everything right
Right inside of me
He knows the miss-marked roads
   and continues down them when it gets cold
I try to trick   to tease
see if he sees
Unentertained he sits quietly
and waits
as I pick at the scabs
off the heavy mask
I've been self forced to have
the ruins of my painful past
in tender shock
to find fresh flesh
skin glowing from the light reflecting off him

Thankful
for being called out
Thankful he is strong
Thankful for my wrongs he forgives
Thankful for all that now
in here
   gives
the best thing
   I never had

Unstartled

As I retire the running shoes
it's come
the time to stop
and see exactly where it is I've taken myself to
My center
centered
breath calm
at ease
inside this comfortable breeze
It's too sweet to run
You're too special to miss
Time to sight see
rest
be friends with time
tour guide lead
I trust the follow
I'm barefoot now
so take the easy streets

Risky Business

And as it's said
The Girl once turned off
switched on
adjusting to new light
Can you trust
that I trust you
and will view all of you
weighed out
in muted truths?
No more dress up day
or wearing the cloak
when I look
unveil what you fear to expose
Indeed
it's the only way I can go
Proceeding in forward motion
can only be impeded with fear
Fear not me then
If it's honesty you dish me
I can stomach it
Stand vulnerable with me
Let it rip   let it go

New Year's

Wild without being tamed
wet but still tight
right without you being wrong
bent but not broken
soft and still strong
truthful yet mysterious
there through hard times to witness
give you my love without losing myself
trust you but also trust me
be thin yet still curvy
be still but not silent
courageous with no ego
to let go
    without getting lost
All this I aim to achieve
while also hoping it stays a mystery

I Can't Enjoy This

now that I know what we've done
I did the best with what I knew at the time
I was single
I thought you were on similar waves to becoming mine
and we went into hiding
protecting us both
In doing so
we neglected the pain
on the lives we left searching to gain
Well aren't we successful?
We tore them apart
We were selfish and careless and what's even worse
is we called this love
How disgusting we are
We deserved to be left
left to feel badly
We cannot comfort each other
because in quiet honesty we blame one another
What was a beautiful dream
left us in the ruin of reality
I cannot enjoy this
knowing all the hurt we have caused
So if at all a token
to the ones hurt in our journey to nowhere
know we are not happy
and we alone with each other cannot bear
I leave now
in the wake of the mess
I am so pathetic and weak I can't let myself rest
The guilt tugs at my tired eyes
I'm sorry for all deceit in disguise
I can't undo all that was done

Even more sorry
for reaching for love
knowing the risk of hurt I might have done
Back to the shadows of bleak
here I come
Back here I go
in hiding never again to seek
love for myself
There's no love for me
And now with this new accumulated karma
there never will be

Adieu

Pay no attention as I slip through the door
the back door
too coward to show my face 'round you
too weak to see you again
Given the chance I'd do it again
hurt you again
You couldn't get too far
to be too far from company's consequences
If I knew then what I know now I'd do it again
again and again
And I won't stop unless you make sure to lock up
I'm walking out but it's up to you to break the clock
the countdown to back step tango into my pain
Go find yourself a nice slow dancer
and make sure to distract her
as your slipping the key into the door
making sure you lock me up
Lock me up
and away baby

The Raw Honesty of Ugly

And it was beautiful
the way you stripped down and evened us out
merged with my soul
and wouldn't let us
and our sea of possibilities go
I hope there better be a God
if only to reward you
for that day you loved me
You deserve in return wings
to be able to fly safe away
from me

Ending Hymn

I jerk off to it
hum along with it
retrace its every move
look for clues
move with the tune
slow dance with his ghost
drunkenly wave and toast
fill up days stacked over days
try to make new memories
to further the pain
He's irreplaceable
This feeling in my chest
I cling to because it's all I have left
since I left

Type X

I'm the type of girl
who hears rejection
when you say
it wouldn't turn you on to see me fuck someone else
because all I hear is
you don't view me as yours
and someone else being in me
wouldn't be wrong by you anyway
Is that fucked or what?

Rejection
Rejection
Rejection

When will it stop sounding
and feeling that way?

One day

I pray
for the threesome
that feels wrong to partake in

Sex is fucked
and I suppose that's the point in it

I Haven't

I haven't written a poem since you
I assume it to be off writing itself
between the bars of a deserted bird cage
where the roots of vines force onward
growing out to form branches of a tree
the height still left an undetermined mystery

I haven't written since you
not for lack of words or desire
but for now a calmness has swept over me
reassuring my every unwritten phrase is gathered
into packaged quotations

That it is all ok

that we are off writing more stories
living more lives
in glory and flight
gone now
from a world that uses poetry expression
and my pen can rest soundly
knowing we are off out there
like birds taking flight

Dodge

I can't look at him
I'll get lost in there
somewhere between
the past
and future
long ago
and out of sight
All I know is we don't exist here
underneath the moon and neon lights
I know you from some other realm
someone else's history book
I cannot make eyes at you
The chills I'd pay for just one look
took too much from me last time
and threatened all of my tomorrows
and that's why I see you there
time traveler
warning me of my consequences
I will not undo
all the rebuilding that's been done
As you shadow in front of me
with eyes pointed loaded like a gun
I hold the bullets
You stand attention as revolver
I refused to accept
as you aim into beaten sorrow
I'll dodge this the way I did the first time
freeing out barely alive

Hinge

I know something
I sense you
yet not brave enough to dream a gaze near
Not yet at least is what I am sensing in you
Dear
you are youthful
but your power is timeless
You know things
I sense in you
you have yet to confirm you know
Sweet philosopher
artist
music man
I feel when I speak you fight the sensation of being drawn in
You are right there at the tip of my tongue
the completed sentence
that without you would go my lifetime undone
You feel it in your ancient wisdom
but your youth crutches you back into a doubtful state
Hush lover
Feel me sink into you
like worn leather to newborn skin
You are the youngest old man
I have been blessed to more than meet
I am meeting you again
We are doing this again sweet pretend stranger
I know you
Stay very still
Do not spook your own shadow
as you see me reflect inside of it
Become dumb
Forget this earth's language
Steady now stay with me

(as if you had a choice anyway)
inside the moon
marriage with tradition of the sun
Let everything you learn now be undone
Look at me only when your eyes are shut
Laugh with me only when our lips are mid-pillow fight
Intertwine with me
and watch the distinction of legs blur into each other
Soul mate
Ah, ease into that sweet truth
Remember me now
that forever paused only temporary outside living
complimentary jigsawed puzzle seduced contrast half
Life's rawest meaning
is here inside this crucial meaning
Forget me not
forever more
Quiet yourself to unlock a little more

Bridge Over Moat

I met you out on the edge out above the city lights
I met you after climbing up and out of struggles
moments before incline
I met you at this crossroad
this pivotal moment before taking flight
The moon was being chased off by the sun
and with the dawn rose our fate
both in trains but separate freights
passing our reflection off the postmarked plates
You're heading toward my concurred hill
I'm leaning down into your slop
We worked our lives up to this point
to locate each other's X-marked moat

Applause

I like him
He says he likes me
I know because history repeats itself
We are already done
So I feel nothing inside the lean-ins of embrace
nor of tomorrow's prewritten fate
I hate this
(but I like him)
I like him while I wait for the hating of him
He is an impressive actor
as he recites stances I know he's won awards for
I deserve a reward for bothering at all

Rotation

They stop in sometimes to throw you off

sometimes for dinner
usually the sex

for no particular reason
other than your name in the Rolodex came across their desk

and they recounted the last time

but subtracted the drama

and figure "fuck it"

they've got nothing to loose
(because it's only your pride that appears on the dice)

and they toss 'em out

and score in any combination

In the Distance

She is weeping
She is selling her puberty under a bridge
In the distance she is banging
her head recalling the first time she bled
She recalls the adults who dumped onto her fragile body
the pressure to keep returning
the self-taught self-hatred tolerated
how they came first
but never fast
In the distance her body dances professionally
but up close – her eyes: frightened amateur dens
vacancy signs and silent cries
Oh, the disconnected distorted distance
leaves her parents arrogantly praising and praying
inside a house over the bridge
their daughter waits for prayers to be answered in
but they keep their distance
and God never showed
as she distracts her horror by looking into
every blurred car, white and fury red
A driver in a station wagon
takes a swig of pills
and drives relieved over the bridge
and the little girl thinks, " Why not me? Lucky him"

Forget Me Not

And she looked up at the stars and they shined only on him
illuminating a future to shine forth in
She packed up her past and buried it at the sea
as they set sail into the life that was the only one meant to be
They stood naked with scars and lusted over
every smooth and stitched-up curve of their lovers' bodies
for it protected the souls determination
to survive through the waiting years
and like a beaten starving dog
make his way back home

You are my only home

The only sanctuary I could ever trust
after years of being shut off
tricked   misguided
and locked in a cell
with a movie screen playing nonstop
man's intentional cruelty

I thought myself mad
to sit through it still
clinically crazed to hold hope inside my straight jacket

I believed in you
though I had no promises you existed

You have proved God still exists
I was so close to done in

You found me with a rope
a gun
a pill bottle
over a cliff

You found me in the last possible moment
I could have been found

Dramatic entrance
worth the painful buildup

I Remember

I remember when my youth turned chilly
and all the roses turned to thorns
All that once invited me
trained me to distrust

The fragrance of my mother's kitchen
replaced with a breeze of emergency
as though the quiche went up in flames
the surveyors listed at the scene
a rotted assortment of dollar-menu maggots
holes punched out and the leaky faucet rust
a baby book without captions and the smiles all ripped off

Nothing safe was left around me
All the children had grown up
Looking back to yield the warning
would change nothing
The time will always come
    time out eventually let's up

Don't Prostitute Your God to Me

I pay only in sums of cheap thrills to wind you up
Religion should be as secretive as a woman's weight
The healthy ones are as obvious
as are the starving
as are the fat
as are the born-again yoyo dieters
as are the bulimics   alcoholics   vegetarian hypocrites
If I'm not dining at your dinner tables
get out of my kitchen
get off my scale
I bullshit it at negative 20 anyway
It's as real as the pounds of saliva you spit
trying to convince yourself
    by convincing me

What It Will Do

Love won't promise you success
but you will never again be stuck on survive

It won't come without risk
but every one of those risks
weigh out higher in worth than defeat

It won't promise you food or shelter
but with loneliness half full, the half empty dissipates

It won't fuck you over
but it will break your bed

It cannot, will not, promise you tomorrow
but goddamn it
even a 24-hour party on it –
    that high gets you through life

Dilemma

I don't want to be the person I have to be to win

I can't live with the person I'd become if I loose

And everyday I'm forging a smile
every laugh is suicidal torture

Every hope I stir up in me
replaces itself in disaster

I need help
or I want out

I can't see it any other way

I either beg for change
or I change directions

The line in the sand is my fired ashes

The letters on the grave are my blood and remains

I lay here
a person taken out of

the dream of the life
I thought I once lived in

I Miss My Sister

Life's so hard
and only she's witnessed it die
I'm attending my funeral
under the blood-red sky
It rains down the DNA that unites us
and then the hurricane of circumstance blows it away
So lonely without you
Memories are replaced with time spent feeling like this

All the Futures I Made

The only line that was real
was the line that was drawn
clearly marked upon
a percentage of love that was lacked
because I met you too late and that's the fact
Now all the futures I made, I want them all back
stacked high on the line
so I can't see where all that love kept from me staying intact

Break

He started a case against me
a list
that includes
all the things that once he pardoned me
from being on the list at all
I can't win

November 25

(true date labeled back somewhere between the start of the big bang
and when the universe hit its limit, looped back to figure eight and
started over once more)

I loved you
Inside space I kept like sacraments
hidden with secrets I forgot to forget
alongside dreams
fears, guts spilled over cries never worn as tears
far back before I felt the grooves of being jaded
time-machined into a future I almost let go of believing in

I find myself in the twilight of the transformed
attending funerals of shadows
I no longer puppeteer
the form of watching what must be a curtain rising
on a play I do not deserve to perform in

In every tango story of your days leading up to our meeting
I finish your sentences, you start mine
What seemed a cruel class with no lesson
was all a test of endurance to get to the "wait and see" it all
with rhyme with good reason in perfect order
one grade elevated by the other
experience stacked on repeat
until we learned what we had to – to reach respect
for the war it took to fight for the right to get to you

I've fought through depression
Liars masked as lovers
I've been given, just to have it taken away
I had to feel all of it and so much more to earn you
Every notch in the belt of the tallied-up reward
Like tickets from skee-ball
I'm finally leaving with the scooter instead of the yoyo

Wee

I never feared you
when you allowed me to see you
but when you would turn back
and retreat to old lovers
I lacked on clarity
lost sight of all the reasons
I bought to believe we could work
in a love shared by two
when half of the union is in unison elsewhere
I fear looking in another eye
so I'll walk far behind
only to catch coattail on another man's crazy lustful ride

We Are

You're the bones to my structure
My softness tightens your grasp
Your cold melted my warmth
and my light darkened your glow
We prey the unforgiving by entering their solid frozen snow
We cannot awaken what hasn't first been put to rest
so we pierce them with eyes shut
to respect the restless damned

Inside every wing sways possibilities of flight
but to take off the dark
we must embrace the white
and the softness must harden to be able to break a fall

We are the lovers
We are the last of them all

Shelter Me, Lover

You grasped me in your pillowed arms
blanket of kisses
then left me back on the outside again
I offered you my final fight
I wanted flight so badly
I pleaded for it to be
you and me and me and you and a list of names
of the little you-and-me's we would birth into a small family
So quick it came
yet the race was won by the take away
I mapped out my heart
left tape to repair it
but you fell on every X-marked pitfall
And now I'm left
with the landscape and no you
with gold still protected by fears of being left out at sea
And there I be
left where found
drowning in the blue
    of what's left of you

It's Expired

The charm
the outfits
the patterned dates
the awe
the attention
the newness
the thrill
the bedroom
the desire
the outcome

We passed our date two dates ago

If we push our luck
we not only will be sharing delusions
but chunks as well

It was a good short run
You made everything better times a hundred plus one

But one more day past
this thing that can't last
and we will be shittin'-sorry
for dining on September in February

Over the Mountain
and Through the Dawn

And the green-eyed girl looked deep
into the boy with the soft brown eyes light
and honored what outshined their love
Praise was given to the man, the infant
the child on his death bed
The legacy only a quarter yet lived
of the green-eyed girl's one true love
His soft brown eyes melted all ego, pushed away pride
and if honesty could sing
a symphony played through her teeth
as all the words she stretched into her vessel to speak
flowed like a river of salted tears
wept for the release of self
And in pounded down a hurricane of grace
for she had learned to love
not to receive love in return
but just to love another
the way no other lover before had deserved
She kissed her boy and gently released his wings
demanded he set flight
into the open sky of night
because this was the best it ever could get
She would not risk another dawn
and the possibilities of it all turning wrong

The Viewing

Some people may never see the struggle
the tears shed at night after exhausted hours are spent
in the dark with my knees held up to my chest
my head down to my heart
my stomach in knots while guts ripped apart
tense and alone
suffering in silence
agonizing in fear of losing relationships that define me
and make living worth the while

No
Some just see me in the morning behind concealer
to hide the circled grey swollen rings under my eyes
They buy into the smile that is selling them lies
They look no further
because it's uncomfortable to imagine
that this girl going through turmoil goes home
to a house made of matchsticks
and whose troubles run like kerosene

I hope they like the red lipstick
because I'll be wearing it at the viewing
as they view the review
of a blind-eyed bad reaction
the last satisfied passion
point made under my breath
leading up to this death
caused by the sinister tongues full of vomit
full of pleasantries
that rub off in your face
Now I'm blue in the face
Oh, not much a disgrace
Don't show up at all, because you're already too late

‹ You

Your loyalty to her deprives us of further intimacy
and insisting she always be a part of your life
will lead to assuring a part of me
is always excluded from yours and you in mine

So this is our max
our limit
and I'm sorry, dear

I'm in search of the eternal quest
the limitless limitations of deep

I love you now as much as I ever will
Because of your restrictions and conditions
I am leaving
to remain free

I love you
You
You
more than

us

Chalkboard

It's sad to watch the decay of something fast
I thought I was taught
it should be slow
It should come with warnings
and signs of symptoms of defeat
I thought it should feel ready
but it burst into every dream
I'm not ready, I'm not ready
but ready is all I must be
because it leaves you with no choice
and the more you resist
the more punishment is tallied up your way

Arm's Length

I'm having a hard day
I no longer can turn to you because you are so cold

You used to be soft
warm
this landing place
arms hairy and strong

Now you're away

and I don't miss you at all

Dammit

Again
and again and again

Fuck this

I can't stomach to witness
one more disillusion

one more time to attend a premature funeral to a love affair
that ran off the course

It all really ends, doesn't it

They stop seeing your beauty

You wear thin
(but never thin enough)
and all sweet nothings lose their sweetness
and you are left with nothing
but guilt shame defeat

Every fucking time

Nothing lasts
not even my relationship with myself
That too in time will pass

And I will have no say as to when I perish
Just the same to say
I am passively watching this love slip, fade away

Think About It

Society spends far too much time focused
around the victims of temptation and protecting the tempters

The prostitute who has a three-day notice
hung on her front door
if not strictly for survival
would never attach this address to her license ID

But she's got a small studio
against all odds, held the family in place

Two small children squished in there
hungry with demands high enough
to raise the roof through the second story
housing another family's distress

Seven minutes down the highway
lives a family-man attorney
who has provided all that could be bought
to distract the woman he once cared for a lot
And he tiptoes late at night
down the road
and through the door
with a notice attached on it
and a payment on the dotted line
higher than he will leave behind

Sunday Night

What did I do?
We do?
What happened?
You love me not?
So soon?
Too fast
My head is spinning
The future is past
I begged you again to stay
Each time you stipulate less and less to be there
to represent the stay
This isn't the way
it's suppose to be
Love
isn't supposed to feel so painful and needy
and one-sided
and guilty
But I want you
Does it mean that because I suffer through those emotions
I do not love myself
but desire
to own this picture I painted
to my daughter and friends and all
I just don't know the answer
After this weekend
   I'm left knowing nothing at all

October 1st

was your due date

I'm sad because
it's still happening
and this is the most real a miscarriage has ever been
I will forever have to list it under "number of pregnancies"
and under "live births," ignore the tear pillowing

And then they'll give me that damn pitied look
they've given me all day
the "I'm so sorry eyes"
It makes me sick to be so exposed
so fucking ready to zip back inside my skin
where I was doing just fine
before they punched windows into my insides
and I bleed out
stories I had no idea my body intended to hide

Discard

Sometimes when you love someone
you give so much more than they need
that you witness after the unwrapping
the toss and plummets of all that love
spread without value or attachment to the nearest toilet
trashcan
fireplace
with a smile of nonchalance
replacing your attempts to conquer this place with love

I'm Not Interested in the Person You Are Aiming to Become

I am wrapped in fascination
with the person you've been living with
What dark secrets you've been able to stomach
what victims remain nameless
as your name is plagued outside an office wall
Who were you?
Rather than who you think you are
or who you hope to be on the way to becoming
No butterfly ever spawned from a snake
No snake even made it off the ground
No child born rich can ever really understand the poor
and the poor only talk about becoming much more

Who were you
will answer where you are going
as it blueprints restrictions
you are powerless at breaking

Damn Me

For every time I turned down a game of Barbie's
damn me
Damn me if you carry with you my short temper
selfishness   constant anemia carried over to exhaustion
translated to a wee one as laziness or disinterest
Damn me
Damn me every time I turned down
a book
a joke
bath time for two
play time
a game of I Spy
that left me spying from the corner of my eye
a child whose excitement plummeted stock at my choices
Damn me   damn me   damn me
It sped up
came too fast
You grew up and I swore you never would
I swore once I never would
But they got to me
Illusion of demands
on hand
when the hand loosing grip
was the one holding my finger
now stretched to outgrow mine
and tugging and pulling away
from a sad excuse of a grip
Damn me
I should have gotten a grip
of what was leaving as I was just noticing it was there
Damn
me

Every mother knows the moment I am recalling
The pity party of the tally marking
You are there with your child
but you fear not present enough
when all you want in the world is to repeat and replay
Damn me
I want her to ask me again to come out and play

Sometimes You See It
for Whitney

Sometimes you see your toughest friends
finding holes poked through that tuff skin
You see them struggle inside teeth grinding down into a smile
You watch them laugh at the bar
kick their broken-yet-again car
find promises broken
and their suspicions fixed
inside every shot from last week's hit or miss
It seems too unfair to document circles and witness
good people have it so hard
Single moms are lonely
though they receive more love than a childless single woman
The loneliness inside a job well done
followed up with no one around to witness
it's a stale feeling stuck like gut
in the bubblegum suffocating your lungs

48 Hours

And then there was that weekend
we spent doubled over in your bed
I was miscarrying our children
You were like a blanket of protection
    the only shot you'd get at a fatherly redemption

We'd wake up periodically
I'd watch you get up to adjust the curtains together
(and I still believe to this day that daytime never existed
 on the other side of the window sill)

You'd come back in bed
kissing, pulling and hugging me tighter
like a low but obvious desperation inside your tug
a feeling showing you were scared
that I   that we
were passing away along with this

We'd attempt a few times a book
or sitcoms   or a movie
but nothing would get finished that weekend
except the duration we spent in hopeful anticipation

Prayers, I guess, come with expirations
Hope does perish
and later
we followed suit

And in a sick way
I'd prefer the 48-hour state to stay

That was the saddest
safest
calmest
most violent time
I have ever lived to barely write about

It's the kind of loss that takes a long time to process
and through the process you realize how big it really was
So in a dark way
the loss increases
and I just have few words left along with it to give away
from our 48-hour day

In the South

Every time I miss you so
and feel a tug in my heart to reach out
I remember the way you shamed me in the garden
and pointed out I was naked
When yelling
"Haven't you noticed I haven't once reached out to you
– this is all you – and it always has been"
And I look around
and I am surrounded by snakes and rotting fruit
and you still haven't come back
and I realized you never came for me
I created this hell
I must leave the dream of you
in order to save my soul from rotting
and the sun to fade from inside the belly of the underworld

To a Chair in Hawaii

I stared out into the ocean
The ocean stared back into me
I saw a million faces in the pupil of the sea

It was the one constant motion
a dance steady pity patter
the rising and rinsing of dreams   waving goodbye
echoing hello

It was the one empty chair obstructing my view
It was the obstruction that had me realize
the view I long to hold to is you

It was all of these things distracting me
from being distracted by you
that made me feel
a memory grow
of the things I forgot I was ready to now know

You're my shoreline
You're my quest and designation
You're the bobbing of the waves
You're the twinkle off a reflecting star
You're all of the things people bother to fight for
My passion
home front
right to love and be loved

The waves enslave me
because you are not here to do the tying up

"Here lies another case
of broken heart"

No matter what I end up dying from
I promise you now
while I'm still coherent enough to clear record slates
and the coroner's report
my body is already breaking down
my mind is untying
my heart slowing
soul departing
I can feel a contract happening within me
almost every cell in agreement
that this broken heart disease is spreading and still no ease
for the flair up that has claimed lives since the mark of time

If I die of cancer
it will be because my body attacked itself
to punish it for pushing you away
If death be in a car crash
it will be because I was playing a song
that caused my vision to go wrong
blurred with running tears
retracing the lyrics and outlined years
If I slip away in my sleep
it will be because I decided to stay put
inside my dream of you
If by bullet   by rope   by bottle   by drug
take fingerprints
off the finger that is reaching out stiff
for the cure that never came back in time to save her

People Are So Painful

Without fail
to know people well
means to dangle off the edge of earth
burning your toes on their fires
 and join in their lack of warmth
Stay away when you start to feel it
bubble up inside your heart
Before you allow that love to spill over
complete then your obituary
condolences of aborted center parts
and brace yourself for the thrill of the kill
the sensation of watching how much they are eager to steal
And, oh, they will take
that vulnerable love induced state
when you offer what little you never had left to give away

Fishing

Have I lost my touch
or I am I just noticing the void of your grasp
Oh, originality
who resurrected you anyway?
The intention is being distorted
with the only words I've learned to relate them in
Raping the violence from the start
wouldn't take away the loss that you aren't
Chicken or farmer
egg
or breakfast
both simultaneously being birthed
inside messed up 'ol me's head

To Nobody (all million of you)

When I think of who I long for
and try to pin it down
where the location of the anchor is held down
a million ghosts pass through me
The haunting truth I am now believing
is that I have spent countless nights
cooped up in a cage of grieving
The lack of meetings
from the ones
who must have been the one
I missed out on
while enjoying the living
who are underground where our lack of love got buried
I miss all the ones I missed out on
This is to you
To nobody
all million nobodies
from another nobody
you'll probably never know

Ring Toss

I promised never to hurt you again
I kept that promise
today
I made that promise to myself
as fiercely as I meant it when I gifted you
Today I am married to my honor
I am falling in love
with the gentle pleasing ease into the soft pledge
Cheers
to all the hearts
that will never be broken
and all the tears no longer falling
to the hour glass with grains no longer middle-stuck
to the dusk that with new permission is transcending
into the dawn of the progression that must follow
They say you must first love yourself before you love another
I rebelled against that banter
and through loving
    you freed me

Growing Up

    It was never the belt
    it was the look in my parents' eyes
    the shameful
    desperate
    doubtful
    folds over their softened eyes
    that created a mood of failure
    not in my actions that started this dramatized reaction
    but in the pathetic mess that comes after attempts
    to claim a life no longer up for claiming

The Drugs You Take

Is it the drugs you take
or the lies you make
that has your eyes sinking in
a trap I've fallen hard into a time or two
with you?
It's sinking in like a tornado
Oh, Dorothy, darling dear
you've spooked the scarecrow
startled all color from here
Take me home
click backwards three times
Simpleton
black and white
to trust all your scenery
Inebriate me with leftover paraphernalia of truth

Themes

I just realized
It hit me out of far left field
This energy I've been fanning onto you
is bagged garbage conversation
from someone who you've showed up to reach out through
and I'm punishing the fixer
You're really not all the same
I hope I haven't scared you away
just as you finally came
"I'll do better"
Because you're better
So much better
And I am so much better than broken
if I won't stop for you, I won't stop for me

Life in the Current

is seen through the eyes of a Universalist
fascinated with everything
I'm sitting backseat to my own rhythms
watching the characters swoosh by
in their own particular fashion
(and at times the lack thereof)
I wish to own none of this
that I have grown accustomed to
I yearn for the formless
distractions at bay
words far from getting in the way
I would prefer to be blind
so that my authentic desire could be exercised
to find connections that cannot be caught inside
all that I have learned to label
I wish to emancipate it all
and swim backward into the feelings
the uprising of co-creating
the sum of vast majority
joyously
leaving
aloneness
loneliness
the cell
that we were

Straddling the Noose

I've got the plastic bag
strapped back around my neck
straddling the noose
tied to the umbilical cord of glorified whoring
I will write for you
I will slam the keys backward
hitting my typewriter's knees
that are pleading with me to knock it off
but I'll hammer away
at night and through day
until it stops
the Beggar
the Nagger
the imposing pestering gut-wrenching shrill in my belly
only to gather all that was never intended to cross your path
As I suck it up
as I swallowed it down
I am disturbed most
by your level of unnecessary anticipation
to the elevated waiting
to eat words I still choke on
to quote what I'll forget after jotting down

I Am Not Easy to Surprise

In themes of relationship slides and disenchantment
I have walked my own hand
one more time plus one again
to similar situations
Men
promises we knew damn well were fake
enough to weather repeated offenses

However
the one thing
to really get
and drag me
through deep disengagement
is my heightened level of sincerity
and shock
at my continuing performance of pain
reacting to
exactly all I signed up for

Same War

Been holding back
while holding on
to this restless tongue
that's shooting off as though in war
so relentless but not completely aware
I'm pulling out
while pulling in
my lips, stapled far from both of them,
suture this tattletale
who's been sharing him for the thrill
I swear she's got him in
as I get in
to another long conversation with him
biting off more than enough
to ever crave this verbal interacting
with him and all men after that

Bull Fighting

All the energy spent in earning this hoarse voice
would have been better directed
in beating the animal into submission
The cage is open for you to take the hint
I'd tell you myself
but I've already said too much
that you took the liberty in editing
and setting in stone
I won't accept another package
of remains of my rapped and distorted words
I cut and exposed my center
to be seen, not replaced

As For Me

I refuse to miss the experience due to ego
May my intentions always be the first to greet the knock
May my light and love
include you
even after you've broken all the rules we built
May I never overdramatize the experience
to include myself inside the inventory of broken things
I am invisible
therefore invincible
May I steer clearly near but never crashing into
my neighbor's heart and fading dreams

The Recall

It's settling back in
that old familiar fear supported by repetition
Will I always do this?
Become translucent too soon?
Express and be vulnerable?
Leave it all open to be used
however they want?
Offend you with suspicious approach?
Will I ever relate and be seen and fit into someone again?
And if I do
will that hurt too?
The way it did before?

Grade C

You took the words
and not only misquoted
but left out essence itself
I feel raped from intention
stripped of all I have ever attempted to mention
when in sincere and exposing conversation
I unzipped my chest for your judgments and suspicion
You were supposed to come back empty-handed
but instead fabricated a map
of all the qualities of disenchantment

And They Judge Us

and I definitely attempt to convince
our special   set apart   nature
and repeat my only defense
"You were not there – and if you had seen us –
seen us as silverware – the fit the stares – the calm fire
that eventually I admit did indeed ignite –
but oh, if you saw us laugh...
That was a welcomed side affect left after the smoke
the ashes   the fallen house and absent ambulance"
I miss being understood
but would being seen completely be worth the trade?
The pain
inside the intimacy of our complimentary raw honesty
I was used to the rug being jerked from underneath
and leftover rags hung out to dry and keep me company
I miss your faults
our damaged similarities
the freedom hall pass
we passed equally between us
I miss our talks
You may be the only person I've met
who was interested in all the same things as me
but older
and so I respected you
and looked up to you
but like most heroes
you lied
You lied
You lied
Your saving grace you felt compelled to say three times
"It was but only three times"
It was never the number or content
It was the space wedged between our intimacy

that those three little lies pushed
everything
far aside
leaning back into a shape
that was used to prop you and me closer in view
I miss missing you
I want to want us
but I can't buy into it

I miss being understood
I miss the art in our conversation
the stylish words and animation
our sides of the bed
Yours had the knife
and mine was a candy nightstand under low light
I miss being together while creating separate stories
me peeking up over my notebook full of mediocre writing
to see the concentration on your face
those adorable teeth biting lower lip
I swear I still can remember the taste inside that indentation
And the drawings
My favorite
I loved how we understood each other's vision
and selfishness

More than anything
I really   really
miss your opinions
I trusted you, god dammit
We fit
because we both have chipped surfaces
similar places we were broken
We loved
and destroyed
equally

Transgender

I talk to these new men
inside the language you used with me
and I think to myself
"He'd be proud the way I quote him,
the way I can fluctuate my voice
and create wit from nothing"
I do this to stroke my ego
I always soared to reach the respect I felt for you
You are seven years older
and inside the body I would have chosen if I was a man
When I'm lonely for you
I read their text in your tone
and play for a minute
that you were still waiting for me at home
When I take the long way to their place
I pass by our familiar streets
hoping serendipity has clocked in today
hard at work
but that bitch takes the longest lunch breaks
So, disappointed, I arrive at their address
and go through similar motions to undress
and clench the drapes extra snug
and dim the lights into a hug
and tighten my eyes to recreate the dream we use to make
This is a fucking nightmare
Meeting you was fate's biggest mistake
I feel so set up to now, forced to validate
with every new "Not You"
the next chapter we ditched before writing
This book would be brilliant if I were cross-dressing

Second Thoughts

Left overly exposed and unsafe
is an old familiar state
I haven't entertained in some time
So please excuse my delayed reactions at this time
I was in a tunnel of intention
that revolved around proof and intervention
to what I already saw as your suspicions of me
and the sincerity inside generosity
So to prove yourself right
you took away all words to include in your fight
and read between the lines
whatever you wanted to believe

The Dentist

There are so many stories
you'll never pry from my throat sutured shut
and how low of a dive into a shallow pool for you to demand me
I promise if you read what I already have chosen
twice
and imagine it to be for you
you'll be satisfied
Just because I write
doesn't mean I owe you what's designed as mine
I've rationed out fairly
in the right space
correct time

I don't ask to sniff your underwear
so kindly remove your grasp from my singing storytelling ass

Found Out

They're following me
They're on my tumblr
my Instagram
my Facebook accounts
in my pants
on telephone
in a movie
in the seat too close to me
I can't let them read free over my shoulder
the way I boasted with you
because they will read it so clear
and look at me like the aftermath of car-meets-deer
and I'll have to admit it
and talk them down further than the disappointment
that they are space I am filling
scabs I've been scratching
covered up tattoos
hiding what I've really been saying

It's not you
It's not you

Motherhood

Watching my art create art
walking side by side with my legacy
and a new better version of that legacy edited and redefined
humbled that because of my daughter
I will never die
being eternally grateful and in awe
witnessing a life from the beginning
allows me the opportunity to rewrite
what life itself is suppose to be
and now *can* be:
supporting the female spirit
an inner light and self-confidence
as it glides like a dandelion
and seeds over forgotten corners of earth
Motherhood has placed me in the most honored of positions
to breathe easy knowing
that if I never do anything more
for the ones I intimately love
or for the world at-large
no greater "thank you" could have matched
the weight of my love for life
than to offer the world a better life in return

Blues

I can't stay, you see
I've got this set of blue eyes in my life
reminding me
of all she's watched her mommy go through already
and if I'm not careful, baby
my baby will think this is what happens every time
and I can't stand the guilt
that tugs on the symphony of heart strings
when she asks me, dressed in disenchantment,
"Where do the lovers go after they go?"
And I can't hold her long enough to know
I need to focus
shake off the chip that started to grow into my shoulder
and redefine what I won't put up with next time
Because of those blues
because of the chance she deserves
I cannot give you another one
Because of those blues
your grey has no room
your lines
are out of line
They fall short
of our side marked in the sand
where I now firmly stand
laying on my back
riding animal clouds all around
and into
the two blues that are more important than you

These Gods Are Relentless

the way they shower down uninvited experiences
experimenting
how to push a pull into a bend to break the hole
I'm tired now
and full of all I never wanted
I need time to process before they hit restart
but they keep trying to refresh my heart
I'm not ready
Humans don't work that way
This pain won't go away
with the start of another created day
Clean away
all that they zero in on
before it stains
and takes little by little
all the big things I never offered to the gods

My Misfortune Pays Your Salary

I'll quit tomorrow
because I soared backwards today
far from the state I tried to achieve
What do you know about addiction?
About the struggle to just be all right
to just slick on by
and "hang in there"
feel good enough to bother to try?
Where the hell does everyone else put their pain?
Mine stays trapped with a holding pass
What do you know about fearing
considering and being guilted by death
every   fucking   day?
What do you know about planning out goodbyes?
About the self hatred in your weakness?
About forgetting what living involuntarily feels like?
About doctors shutting your complaints up with a pill
and toasting after with a big fucking bill
    forced you to escape to the high
      just to forget the money you'll never have to pay
      for your own heart attack?
I hope I survive
so I can read
and reread what I'm saying today
I hate this
If I make it out alive
I swear again
    like I did two months ago
      and several years and a decade before that
to try
Fuck body, please try!
To survive

They want to toss another life preserver
really just an enabler
I've been clinging too long
to hit repeat behavior
and reach out to a Never Come Savior
My eye signs vacate
This is not attention getting
just a scratch on the back
to prescribe another month's worth
to pay for the doctor's fifth wedding
Killer medication, Doc
What are you cutting this with? Your retirement plan?
College and big football plans for your children
the ones you would never medicate?
This system is built on a greedy man's intake
When it comes to patience, I'm your patient
because I have no other choice
and you set me up to wait for it
Wait for what?
Another day to be the day?
Another pill to pop away?
Another cry for help
I never got out to say
because I was taught to feel ashamed
for the additions the commercials claimed
would come my way?
Dear statistic:
I'm climbing up the charts
and to be realistic
more like a land full of broken hearts
No matter what the quote from cause of death be
know my poems were all that never got the best of me

I Struggled
with Writers Block Once

After I unsuccessfully helped myself to a fill of pity party
complaining for compliments I got tired of aiming my way
I moved away
far from that old language I fought through outgrowing
and shopped for a better fit
to fit contemporary style and reflect some serious age
I stopped talking like I was five
and rewriting stories I talked into a grave
read a book
took a walk
and left all I knew alone in a drastic way
And softly
without familiar force
emerged a new voice
that was always there
expanding in the space I gave for watering
It takes a lot to move into
what we are meant to become
authors speaking through whistling dentures, aged tongue

My Parent's Dog Is Moaning

Their other dog has been on its fourth leg for some time
and all I can think is,
"Fuck! I'm not in the mood for this!"

What the hell has my life come to
where the sounds of a dying
and grieving dog
puts me off?

If only everyone around me wasn't reciting wolf
then when things that actually deserve attention
and condolences
they wouldn't die alone
due to being immune
to all the moaning and death
suffocating us into the balancing act our own fourth leg
Truth be told
I'm jealous of that lucky dog
Why does he get to get out
and see if shit is indeed in store
while I sit here begging to replace his last jump for the ball?
I'm tired of dodging suits and of mundane eating
I'm sick of everyday predictability
Surprise me with death
Not one more breath
Fuck you dog!
It should of been me god dammit
It was my fucking no good turn

Your Socks Filled with Criticism

I'm positive it shouldn't come this way
The road to creativity comes with pain
bleeding for a product spent
long before the book is burned over the internet
where all you critics find your home
to connect and reach out
through a tall hand of cards I gave you to all to own
while I deal with the progress of details
I'm just trying to relate
while you are invested in taking me down
for someone you've never met
only read about
And after all that personal intimacy I shared
you still have no problem bashing me?
Just because I told you my heart's broken
doesn't mean it still can and does break again
    and again
I put it out there as a way of reaching over
an extension of my soul from the lonely human hand
and you slapped it down with the weight of your review
Didn't you read in chapter two
how I'd never do that to any of you?
Summarized before entering
exited before talking
while I forgive you prematurely
you're sticking my pages together with your pre-ejaculation
you busted out over what you've already listed
on a long-ass scroll of all that was not right
Enough of you
in this book
about
me
that person you'll never remember to remember anyway

I Broke You, Huh?

Well, you both are welcome for the foreplay story line
you used on her
and she spoon-fed back
while you fell in love during arts and crafts
Piecing it back together
one   by   one
all of our tragedies
I'll still be here
reliving it again and again
and adding daily to it
new marks on the heart you took to get consoled
Is nothing our own anymore?
Even our pain is stolen
yet not taken away
Nothing's sacred to my old friend and me

Shoreline

I went to the shoreline to let my heart release, sigh and cry
I went to the shoreline to be alone
and hold still to time as it's slipping away from me
I went to the shore to feel sorry for myself
and to hold all mistakes accountable
for whatever it's worth now

An old woman approached me from across the fog
her voice immediately drawing me in like a grandmother's hug

She asked me why I cry so hard
I couldn't speak up loud enough to form words
so she filled in space with presumption
and said after a long pause of hesitation:
"It is because someone has died"

I wanted her sympathy and wisdom
– anything really – so desperately
but couldn't grab the explanation
of how it wasn't exactly one death
but an entire life
that had gone away from me and died
that all wants and needs are being buried
and accepted as an investment I never really cashed in

So many have died
and gathered for my reason for coming to the shoreline
particularly the fog in the air
and the silver from the moon and the old lady's hair
and the wind that collects the tears off my face
and all of the memories I'm casting off into space

Night One

It's lighter than despair
but far more serious than disappointment
It is the point in the path
where one of two branches
has moved on
Thriving
growing
and turning brilliant healthy greens
while you are just waking
and allowing honest self realization
to become one with the day-to-day
of   today
It hurts
but expectedly
it reopens wombs you've been missing the map to retrace
and by sun break
by the bow into the night
it vanishes and it is the new kind of gone
the kind that comes without threat or game
It's gone
because it really fucking is this time
and he's moved on
and you better start clawing up that sleeve
to see if anything has pardoned you
to comfort enough
to last
if nothing else
this first night

Empty Arena

This is the kind of night
that I am positive will be contemplated into my golden years
the kind where
no matter how sincerely I handle it
it is shaping me
in what fashion
or light
is still yet to be seen
but there is no way
in any answer to "how"
that a loss inside my heart
could not account for years of private-eye loss
being exhausted
and exchanged
for "could have beens"
by new memories and pet names
No
I chose you
and regardless of your moving on
I'm stuck in the most drawn-out quicksand
holding onto confusion
and all I thought we were
while he
is out with the "what really is"
he really is

Warning

Don't follow me for I am cursed
The state in which I've stayed since birth
when descending between
a whack job junky's knees
is the start of the root of all problems it seems
Do not quote me
I speak in tongues
in tons of layered manure laid out in front of me
Do not touch me
You will burn
from the intensity that only fuels up the flares
and fires to soften the burns
Do not come with me
wherever it appears I am heading
It   is   a   lie
Do not love me
My heart's piggybank has been shattered, stolen, sold
and stuffed into Swiss accounts
found out and sent off to hell with no chance of bail
Do not
whatever you do
read this and think
it has anything to do with you
or anything to do
with me
and that time you did follow me

I Am Poet

I am
a poet and I know it
See what I did there?
I rhymed
and softened the harshness
you almost started to read this in
I am a poet because I stay up too late
because I have done drugs
and seen things sober I've tripped on
to the point of living with a debilitating crutch
because Social Security doesn't recognize this
and pay each month
for time to walk out of that mental wrench
I am a poet
I am a poet because I can't figure out
where everyone else stuffs their pain
So I, with thoughtful, slow, intentional thrusts
move my words into smaller
more highlighted sentences
because for my cut-down-on-pain diet
that seems to work
I am a poet because mystery loves company
and a happy heart must boast and birth jealousy
I am a poet because we all give some title to someone
and if I call myself this first
it displaces less fortunate titles
other titles
almost titled to me
I am a poet
in short
to beat you all to the punch

Dear Denny

We were quite possibly the only two people
who play James Taylor on the way home
from a punk rawk show
the only ones to laugh for 20 minutes over whistling
and consider our most romantic dinner
to have taken place at Denny's at 3 a.m. on a work night
You were worth all the exhaustion the next day
and all the days after that
We laughed so hard that night
I'll never forget where I lost it...
And hearing James Taylor resurrects your ghost
from the period before it all tumbled south
That night evened the playing field
and gave me what I needed
to validate reason inside broken days
I'll leave you there
next to the cd
the cigarette ash
and menu stained by the syrup for your pancakes

I Cannot Convince Another

what happened between us
and I am broken hearted, sure
that you don't feel the heat
of protection when you speak of me
and the things we, in hindsight, survived
But when I think of you
in my vessel, it's true
that there's a longing that runs as wide as all rivers combined
and I've choked through the "tries"
and held tight to our last goodbye
never giving it up, after hanging up
just standing by your flight
as you fly by
and there you go
you are off
Farewell and good luck
I won't compliment you further with guilt
or point out all the missing you don't feel
but I will
steal a smile
a kiss and a wish
and stay inside memories you gave up
You were the hit
and I was the miss
Shooting star
you happened only a few times where I could see you
and I reached out to feel you
and be a part of your quickening glory
as you whizzed by on your way
to where you actually were going
while I
along with my roof
admired and gazed

recapped and repaid
you
for hanging over our brains
and filling them with enchantment
lasting days
after meaningless days

Time Flies When You're Swatting

You left me deserted in the warmth of being right
surrounded by shadow-casting skyscrapers of wrong
What does it matter without the echoed chatter
relentless company to my tagging along?
Alone, muzzled in my rebel head
it feels like I traded all life
to march with the aftermath of death
What do crossing points matter when the bridge burns
and no longer gathers a withering string from me to you?
I cut myself off way too soon
I'd rather bite my tongue and say it was you who won
than be dragged and punished another day
for all those listed things I proved
just to prove that I'd eventually run you away

Some Are Born Mid-Soar

in flight
a height that lifts the bar inside the quiet corners in us all
Powerful in silent example
and loud in happy painful laughter
excepting
because free
walking alongside the great arch of disappearance
the true expansion of our own mystery
taking shape large enough to examine now
Jeremy had that mystic gypsy spirit that left a soft calm
with everyone in his wake and presence
He was so great an energy
now broken up
disappeared in each of us who are left to carry on

So now
with the gift of his love's incarnation that births within us
the expectation to carry out his joy and his mission
returns to do a greater good for all we meet
from our todays and tomorrows

We gain from every give
inside every hush
we can soak in the vastness that he is now a part of
His communication will take the shape of intuition now

Thank you
for the mingled, ricocheted conversations smiling your smile
staying forever our muse of creativity and inspiration

We were lucky
to have had your physical presence on this earth
and now forever grateful to keep you encapsulated
in our own private journeys
to our own great mystery and disappearance

What do we do with our pain?
Give it away
in food for the homeless
in patience inside a restless day
into the appreciation
of every connection we continue to water

Give it away all over
just as Jeremy shared
and gave himself completely
to the experience and love of it all

It Happens That Way

We'll die in the middle of sentences
births and alongside more deaths
No matter how it happens
it won't be completely unordinary
and that makes it all the more mysterious and unique
We will die the same
eyes shut, then never to flutter again
We will however not live the same
and that will make all the difference
The similarities in our exits
are to comfort us as our individuality
spent in designing the circumstances of our days here
the ways in which we choose to fill them up
and the things we leave behind
inside the ones still telling our stories after we go
Be mindful that the tone
the only author of your story
relays every encounter and every chapter
of your one and only
collection of days

I Am Still Afraid

and I am ready to admit it
I found it   pinpointed
It's there and now that I see it
everything else is getting adjusted and coming in clear
It is as I should have always suspected
feared again
always rooted in
the holding back of the process I claim I want possession of
fear that if I try
I can't say it didn't work out because of lack of trying
I will have to marry guilt with shame
if it doesn't work out
fear that she   they   all the *theys*
will penetrate right through me
and figure me a fraud
What if I dig too deep past all the comfort
safe landings or cheerful nothings I've used
to build up a character
that actually   might truly   not exist?
What if I am wrong
and I was special
but fear and the power I gave it
never allowed me the chance?
Ah   I shall end with that
What if I am wrong?

Now back to the balls to find out

QUOTES

I Said That

I quote because I want to be quoted.

We miss so much due to fear of missing it.

How original of him to be so typical,
and I play the supporting part of the crutch so well.

These roles are as timeless as the carvings on the stage we dramatize them on.

I see it and you and me in it, and you every time I shut my eyes. We exist in hues of red.

Live as brave as a lion but humble enough to befriend a dove.

People are inherently good. I know this to be true, because I see the pain inside unsettled hearts when we break our birth right and act against the nature of our soul.

Moving up the social scene where I come from only means doing more drugs with a smaller group of people.

Being loved meant being the one who provided the drugs to the selective. And being popular meant knowing where to get the loving from.

A quote a vegetarian might pervert:
If only we were who we present on a first date or to our grandmother (on our mother's side). Those representatives are nowhere to be found after you've been fucked over. After that, the salesman's face is blown off exposing you — Packaged Raw. (And no one dines with meat uncooked.)

Everyone has an equal right to be well. The poor, the rich, wicked and deep. If our bodies are not working at maximum capability, then we are all destined to join the mass funeral of progress, stunted in a sick system of the have-nots.

Compassion has finally wept its tears over my soul and potted me in a foundation ready for growth.

We are the kind of flame that burns you during the strike of a match. We are eager, but ill-equipped for longevity.

Sometimes you are better off choosing to nibble on daydreams than to risk food poisoning from the hungry day's demands. Stay in bed until you are starving enough to withstand the nausea of a man.

For control freaks:
If you accept chaos, then you expect it. And even in random rotation, you have now transformed it. In some sort of order.

And on other nights,
the absence of clouds
is replaced by a lonely hinge
on a velvet door
with a million peepholes.
I wonder which side is the house,
and if both sides are looking in?

It's never been that I am under the delusion of thinking I know more. I am, however, spellbound convinced I am the only one who makes complete sense.

It's always sad when an artist of any fancy is caught being judgmental. It's a peace sign and the flip of the bird, hands in constant rotation even in turns.

My point takes the bridge.
Your point prefers the tunnel.
We are fighting to get our points across
missing that we are there
as we parallel each other.

You watch it happen and I feel nothing towards it. Love; the point of no ownership, the moment when you are gazing without judgment or thought, witnessing in splendor and awe.

Attempting to solve a problem by putting a rug over it only fans the fire. How are we to clean up the mess if you hide it? If I cannot see the challenge, you along with it, remains unseen.

Sometimes you are needed to play a role in someone else's life and that does not mean they owe it to you to play a part in yours. Gaining from an experience can come from the unattained.

Wait!
Where are the exits again?
I was too busy admiring the art on the pamphlet
labeled *IN CASE OF DISASTER*.
I need the escort to show me the way out
that lead me in.

If you list timing as a reason you're in love, then I will celebrate it with the same pizzazz I do when noticing my oil needs to be changed.

You're stuck wondering if people change. While I'm listening to you, I'm recalling that you asked me this the last time you had a relationship end. The answer's on the tip of your tongue. If you'd only swallow it instead of fixate on it like tasteless gum.

They never come back, do they?
And you never find that happy ending . . .
Or maybe you do?
But it's when it's ending
and by then no longer happy
because there is someone left asking
if there is ever an Act Two.

I promise to pretend if you promise to forget.

Set them free after you love them. You own nothing earthly. Taking will only weigh you down on your journey to take flight.

My beautiful daughter started kindergarten today. All floating stress that had been drowning me is left now for the fishing out.

We are mermaids! she says
and that's the only depth I want left.

I want to believe so badly that you are worth believing in. I want to believe this belief more than I want to know the reality I base beliefs in.

Having the person who is breaking your heart
tell you they love you
must be how a patient feels
when the doctor announces
the only way to save your life
is to cut your insides out.

I can't be with you, but I have *got* to be near you!

Guilty of overkill in the first degree.

How many lies does it take to get to the center of the truth?
How many clicks of your heels to turn your world from black and white, back to color?
How many licks to get past the mediocre and bite into the center of goodness?
How many times does Bart Simpson need to write on the chalkboard until they realize people don't change?

Marriage is riskier than having a redhead. You'll likely be accused of far more bizarre things than the milkman being the cause of the DNA hair strand.

I might not be the type of girl you bring home to mom, but Daddy will fucking *love* me.

If a guy hasn't ripped one around you after a month, he's planning on holding a lot more than broken wind from you. And never trust a silent fart.

I worry I don't worry enough about things others worry about – a social retardation rooted in misdiagnosing what is universally the same.

Stigmata: we all bleed crimson red.

The other side of the face on the coin is the painful realization after meeting u, I was missing something before. How ever am I to return partial?

Holding onto my feelings for you is as useful as sweeping up leaves on a windy day. I can't pick up what the sky insists on falling down. I am like trash going into a bag with a hole in the bottom. I give my words and feelings for you, but they fall through every time.

And just like that the spell was broken. And I looked through the mirror made-up reflection and saw you for the first time. And realized, we have nothing in common. The clock struck midnight and cautiously I took the flight as far as I could flee from the shadows of what came to be and all that was never there between you and me.

I didn't come with a pause button.
When you leave me to get lost inside your head upon arrival there is no rewind.
I just kept on going goodbye

Somewhere between out of words and biting my tongue

When you let me down I reach up to him.
But in this equation
I start where I begin.

You fucked with my head
when you made love instead that day.
That wasn't the plan.
We were supposed to be animals on the floor.
Instead you jumped right in my heart,
had me trembling, begging you for more.
You were supposed to be cheap.
Now I can't afford to lose you.

Every day since has been as hard as walking through the nauseating filth of the hell you deserve to be rotting in, fuck you!

Dearest lovers,
be kind to the bodies that trust their love
in the hours of your actions,
actions inside faithfulness
or you could find yourself buried
in the heart of a raging storm,
swelling of broken sharp pieces
you carelessly littered over your torn out heart.

I'll be the book
and you'll be our songs
and they'll watch us like a movie
as we drive along

Getting to heaven ain't easy
It's all about who you know
and it's been long since I rode with angels.
The preachers turned mute 'round me.
Down here in this shapeless purgatory
all the devils I came to know have gone
and heaven's too far for me.

When it comes to people,
you shouldn't need to break something
to figure out what it is or how they work.

You fucked the living corpse out of me.

And all things go back
to the things they never came from at all.
When we die we lose form, turn in with dust and wind.
Who am I
if *I* am strictly leased?
Where in the policy does it state cancelations
and special dates of importance reminders?
I don't see the *to do* in what returns back to returning.

Only a writer could see this ugly world, see the deaths, the abuse, the unfairness, the hopeless attempts of the loveless lovers, and the poorest in heart inherit all the wealth and still report back poetry.

And wouldn't it just go to show validity in the fight. I never remembered all you said to me because what was left unsaid were the only words recalled, recited, redundant, mocked, repeated, now dead.

==Just because you recognize you were wrong==
==does not warrant you a hall pass==
==to skip through the emotional damage you cause those==
==still in class studying you.==

Skiba made the clavicle sexy.

People can be mean.
It's the worst when they aren't trying to be
because that kind of meanness has no leader,
no start to follow with an end.
It's a run-on sentence leading to no-guilt reflection.
It comes and goes to the giver.
To the receiver, it echoes and aches.

Wanna see how fast I can peace out? Try gaining attention through jealousy. I am the most passive competitor you will ever challenge-proceeding greed.

Your silence nagged me all night. Your void left me full of loss. Remind me again to forget you.
I feel used when you don't use me.

Divorce court. It's every stream of consciousness manifested into a nightmare.

Love will not fuck you over, but it will break your bed.
I'm so simple – with you it's simple – and you simply choose to be shady – and so it's simply lost – and you passively watch it slip – the way you passively committed to showing up at all.

I'm sorry for any pain knowing me caused you. I am even sorrier that leaving another one sorry was my tailored remedy.

His solid void crosses paths with the soft lift.
They were held up by only this.

No one worried about Bukowski and his loneliness and his whores as drugs. So don't concern yourself with my wellbeing as I allow you to page through only one specific part of my diary.

There comes a time everyone must ponder what it means to be "Revved up like a *duce*."

It's 2 a.m.
I'm Googling:
are dragons and unicorns friends?

He must be the one.

I woke up.
I found my say out of the bind.
It took nearly a year and bits and parts of my mind
but I'm content with what's left
and with what's all been gained.
I'm the owner of my own life,
no longer at the mercy of mercy to rein.

To meet you
at dusk I must
first leave all baggage behind
depart from the day
embark into night
abandon all plans
that waiting in stand-by demands.

I'm never flipping a Lucky ever again.
Fortunate ones come from lungs that rest
like Clinton, never inhaling again.

And if you just so happen to stumble upon her . . .
and she just so happens to lock eyes with you
and shy away smiling . . .
what would you be prepared to do about it?

The slew of storms passed and you bailed before the rainbow.

Excerpt,
from a poem I already wrote about a man I'll never know:
We met during an avalanche – our lives were being melted and formed – and before you could see the new melted earth formation you set sail and wrote of us only in our times of winter – never glancing back once to see the beautiful scenery of spring and sunshine. I saw it all go down and will never forget the way you looked with your back to me sailing into another storm.

I hope I come out of this
and become the person
I've been faking to be all along

Remember the time I found the hair tie
and you hugged me
and I stopped being sad
and just
stayed?
That was great.
Last night was the opposite.

People hurt.
They will hurt you.
You will hurt them.
If you try to change this,
you will hurt you.

It really hurt my feelings
that you didn't think to wish me a Happy Mother's Day.
It feels terrible
and mean
coming from you
considering . . .
It still bothers me tonight,
which is why I'm texting it.
I just cannot imagine being overlooked in those regards
after all this time spent as the holding of high regards.

Love the love
not the title
or entitlement of it.

Taking inventory of all the unsaid phrases
passed up in the sweetest chapters pages
I recall the day my heart sank
weighted down for the sake of all I believed in
and a swoosh of relief started a calm fire beneath
fanning and living off the protection of our fate.

I am made up of a human shell that moves and trades
memories with motives under the vise of time and experience.

One day
I won't be surprised
at how surprised I get
when . . .

Way to miss the message
highlighting and jotting
commentary on my spelling
my distance between words
and the time it took to
let the go leave from interest.

Dear god, there must be a safer distance,
some sort of mile recommendation
for the defective elevation in some of your creation.
I can't swim inside the stream.
Humans stun too fast for me.

Enough calling me out.
Just because you love me
doesn't give you the right to rape all
to expose a hole in the story.
Fuck you for showing up with nerve enough to unnerve me.

A love letter in your locker doesn't make you a fucking writer.
What happened to the tormented souls
who had to live with ripped-out teeth
and loose toenails to crawl into your speaker
just to meet her?
Sometimes you give it all to strangers
only to be left with fucking nothing.

. . . and on other nights, you have to remind yourself, as convincing as you conveyed, how little a fuck you give but oh, what you'd give, for one more of those little fucks, to have the strength to forget, all the way over and again.

There are some things
I'll never get over
never grow out of
      alkaline trio
      Bukowski
      hot sauce on everything
      self-destructive behavior
      and you.
You apply with all of the above

I said that.

Made in the USA
San Bernardino, CA
09 March 2020